The enchanted Christmas book

Martin Jonas

Martin Jonas

The enchanted Christmas book

Come with us to the land of Santa Claus

DeBehr

Copyright by: Martin Jonas Publisher: Verlag DeBehr, Radeberg First edition 2024
ISBN: 9783987273308
Graphics created via midjourney.com With coloring graphics by Lilly Kahle

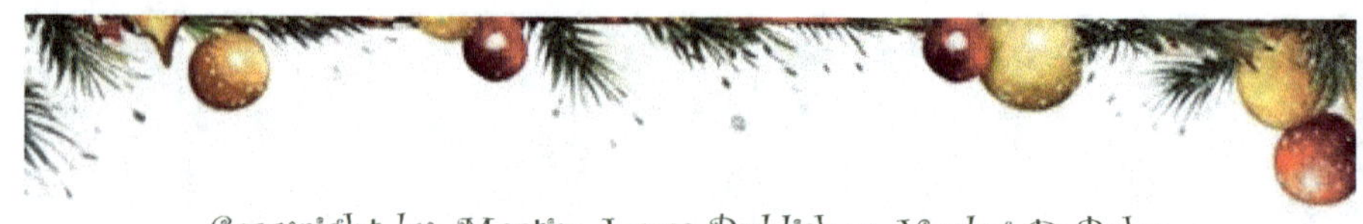

Content

Where am I?

Oh, hello, how nice that you found me! I'm really very happy about that!

You know, I had my eyes closed the whole time. Where I was staying was pitch black. I was alone and very sad. But now I'm in good hands, I can feel that.

You have a nice room, I have to say. Your place is really cozy and so nicely furnished. Much nicer than the dusty, cold place I've spent the last few months in. Or was it years?

No daylight. No warmth. Just a few fat old rats scurrying through the corridors.

But now I am happy because I am with you!
And you know what? The two of us are about to go on a magical journey. But only if you want to, of course.

So, do you want to? Yes?
How beautiful!

But before we set off together, you have to promise me something, okay?
Can you keep a secret?

You know, I'm already over two hundred years old, and no child in the world has ever laid eyes on me. You are the first human child to hold me in your hands. It makes me a little queasy - but I feel I can trust you. Can't you?

So if you can keep a secret, I'd be delighted if you read on and we become friends. But you mustn't tell anyone that I exist! Not even to your best friend. Promise?
I know that sounds a bit unfair, but there really is a good reason for it.

If I can trust you now and you want to be my friend, then please turn the page and just read on.
If you are afraid or know that you are a little chatterbox, just put me aside and stop thinking about me.

Yay! So you're an honest and sweet child! That makes me happy. I had hoped that you would be my friend and help me. Come on, I'll tell you my little secret.

You've probably wondered why I'm such an old book. Or have you ever seen a book older than me?

It all started with the elf Kiru.
Yes, you read correctly. A
funny name, don't you think?

Kiru wrote to me.

To be more precise, Kiru, the
Christmas elf, even invented
me.
He wanted to preserve the spirit
of Christmas for eternity.

And what could be better suited
for this than a beautiful book in
which the magic of Christmas is
written down in all these fantas-
tic words?

As I said, I was simply left on a shelf in a dusty and cold place. My only companions were rats.

I don't know how I ended up with you, though. You have no idea either, do you?

But maybe I'm with you because you carry the childlike magic of Christmas within you? When I look at your watch, it makes me a little sad. At this time of day, Kiru was always hopping around the desk with his warm star cocoa and telling me the greatest stories.

I haven't seen Kiru and the other elves for a long time.

Santa hasn't had me on his desk in his huge office at the North Pole for a very long time either. And I have to tell you... Santa's office is three times the size of your children's room. Yes, no joke! Behind his big desk, the fire blazes all day long in the beautifully decorated fireplace. There are tall bookshelves to the left and right of it, and they are full of books. You've never seen so many books.

And let's not forget the numerous lists of 'good' and 'bad' people.

'naughty' children that our boss, Santa Claus, has to revise every year.

The smell of hot cocoa with cream and baked gingerbread is everywhere.
Contemplative Christmas music fills the room and the gigantic chandelier on the ceiling shines in its warm light, together with the large Christmas tree.

Hey, why are you looking like that now?
Don't you believe me?
Come on then, I'll show you!

Hide yourself!

And here we are already! Welcome to the enchanted world of Christmas!
I lived here for two hundred years. It is a place full of magic and wonder.

But look!
Over there. Quick! You'd better hide behind the tree first.

Before we can go any further, you have to disguise yourself. No one must know that you are here. And certainly not that you are a child from the human world.

People have no place in our world.
It would be best if you could quickly put on a hat to hide your human ears.
Do you have a hat?
I have nothing against the clothes you're wearing right now. It looks cute and funny. Just like the elves.
Conspicuously inconspicuous.
But your ears are invisible. Just human ears. Elves have small, pointed ears, but I'm sure you know that. And now please put on a hat quickly, otherwise we can't go any further.
Wow, that looks cool. The headgear looks great on you.

Now we can walk into the Christmas village without having to worry about anyone recognizing you. And nobody can see me either. Not that I'll make you stand out after all.

Besides, I don't want to stay here in the forest any longer than absolutely necessary. Because I'm a bit scared. I'm not as brave as - ...
Do you know who lives behind the green thicket up there on the hill?

The sandman!
It knows so many stories - and it knows all about you children. The Sandman and Father Christmas know everything about you.

Quietly and secretly, the little sandman sneaks into your children's room every night and spreads the soft sleeping sand. And he's no bigger than you!

With a big smile on its face, it blows the sand into your little eyes so that you can sleep soundly and dream beautifully. But when a child is naughty, there are no dreams. These children wake up the next morning and have not dreamed of beautiful things like the good ones.

The Sandman is also always well dressed. His coat is unique. It sparkles in different colors.

No one ever knows exactly which colors they are seeing, as it is impossible to follow the play of colors. One moment the coat shimmers green, the next red. When the light breaks, it sparkles yellow, or even purple.

Tell me, do you know where we are right now?
Do you have any ideas?
I'm not really allowed to reveal anything specific. Only that we are in the cold north. Where no one has ever been before. Well! Except for you.
You are the first person in this area.
Santa Claus lives here with his hard-working elves. Ah... our cue! Elves. We can't ignore that. You must pretend to be an

elf from now on. Are you going to do that?

Let's think about it...

What do you need to be an elf?

You already have a hat on your head.

You're a little taller than most elves, but that shouldn't be noticeable.

Your clothes are right.

So what else do you need?

Ah! You don't have a suitable name yet!

You know what? We'll just call you Zwölfie! Yes, Zwölfie sounds great, don't you think? You must never forget your name. If anyone asks you, you'll be called Zwölfie from now on.

Come on, let's move on quickly, Zwölfie. And take a look at the beautiful, snow-covered mountains near us. Unfortunately, I can't show you exactly where the Sandman's hut is, because nobody really knows. But don't our mountains look great?

The white blanket of snow lies like delicious candy floss on the mountain peaks all year round. Even in summer, when the sun is shining. But then it's so warm up here that the elves and even Santa Claus himself walk around in swimming trunks.

Santa has a really funny pair of swimming trunks. They are white and have twenty little red hearts on them.

Is there that much snow where you live?

Wait! Once we've walked down the snowy slope, we'll soon come to Christbaumstrasse.
This is the main street that leads through our Christmas village.
It's actually the only road here.
The other streets are small alleys and forks.

Don't forget: You are the Elf Twelve.

And look, over there, to your left! The purple house. That's my best friend Naschie's sweet store.

*Sweets in abundance, the smell of sugar
makes us crumple.
We love the tasty delicacies!
You absolutely have to spread
Naschie's art.*

Isn't his store cute? I helped Naschie with the exterior decoration for his store. I like those lights on the windows. It just looks cozier with the gold and red balls on the garlands.

Do your parents also decorate your home?

Naschie is the coolest elf here in the village, I can tell you that. He has everything your sweet tooth desires.
From delicious gingerbread and marzipan balls to spicy nuts and cinnamon stars. Simply every-thing!

Every year, when the colorful plates of sweets stand under your Christmas tree, shimmer-ing in the glow of the many lights, you can be sure that your parents got all the great treats from Elf Naschie.

Arrived

Wow, how time flies! We've arrived on the main road. The journey didn't seem so long now.

Watch out for the wild sledgers.

These are our postal elves.

They are always a bit stressed so close to Christmas.

They rarely look to the left or right.

And look - up there above the Christmas bakery you can see a little horn on the façade of the brown house. That's our post office. This is where all the wish lists from you children go.

*The post office
is the most important place for
us.
We tighten the postbag strap.
Your wishes
come to us every year, whether
small,
whether large,
we have won. We enjoy sorting
your notes,
but please stop cycling.*

The post office is the central point in our village.

You could almost say: the centerpiece.

We receive millions of wish lists every year.

By the time the mail elves have finished sorting, the next wishes from you children are already fluttering in.

Fortunately, we have had this really helpful pipe system for a few years now.

That takes a lot of work off your hands.

You simply sort the wish lists alphabetically by name and drop them into the corresponding tube.

This well-designed system does the rest by itself.

The best of the best

I talk a lot, don't I? But you're such a good and curious listener. That's what I like about you.

To your left is Naschie's store. You already know that. And to your right is Schnürgel and Josie's house.

Schnürgel works in the toy factory. He's the best toy maker we have. Put a piece of wood in his hand and he'll conjure up anything you want.
The coolest wooden train. The fastest car.
The most amazing table. Simply everything!

His wife Josie works in the tex-
tiles department.
I wouldn't be surprised if the hat
you're wearing on your head or
the shirt are from Josie.
The eleven's clothes are also
from her. The green jackets and
matching shorts took some getting used to for most of them at
first.
However, I personally love the
white and red striped tights. The
elves' legs look like little candy
canes in them.

Who is in charge?

So, what's your first impression of our village? That would interest me. Every day is Christmas here. And the decorating elf Schmückie helps us with that. The only elf who calls the shots when it comes to decorating. An ambitious and very creative elf who sees beauty in everything. He works quickly and conscientiously. Everyone loves and appreciates him and his work. Especially Father Christmas. Schmückie comes up with new decorating ideas every day to make everything here even more beautiful. His work is an enrichment for us all. But quickly, let's move on.

Books about books

Welcome to our library. This is where I have spent most of my life. This is my home, so to speak.

Come in, come in! There's hardly ever anyone in the library. Well, except for Kiru, the elf who wrote me.

Maybe we're lucky and he's here right now.

Oh, I like the smell of books! Old books, new books. Lovely! Do you like the smell as much?

Kiru used to roll through the library on the ladder leaning against the bookshelf. That was great fun for him.

Back and forth. Climbing up and down. Kiru loves books.

But wait a minute! You can't even see the ladder. I can't see it either. Where has the ladder gone?

Let's take a look around. Maybe we'll discover the book shelf somewhere after all.
In this mysterious place you will find everything you ever wanted to know about the Christmas village. All the thoughts, all the secrets and all the Christmas preparations are

revealed here. Recorded in writing. But only the elves can open the books and read the writing.

So, have you found the ladder yet?
No? Maybe Kiru? No?

I haven't seen him either. But he must be somewhere, this little rascal. Where could he be hanging around?
It's best if I describe Kiru to you first so that you can get an idea of him.

Kiru wears a vest with a small red bow tie or a red scarf around his neck every day. He is three centimetres taller than the other elves. At 120 centimetres, he is the tallest elf of them all. Kiru likes books and loves playing cards.

Eye-catching, chic, elegant and witty, Kiru has style and taste. You could almost say the vest is Kiru's trademark.

When he needs a little break, he goes into the stable with the reindeer and lies down in the hay to sleep.

Have you just the the same thought as I did?

Do you think we'll find Kiru with the reindeer?

Okay! Then we should definitely go to the reindeer stable.

In the stable

Here we are! Here we are looking after the reindeer of the
Santa Claus. Quite a big stable,
don't you think? Very cozy too,
isn't it?

Here live: Dasher, Dancer,
Prancer, Vixen, Comet, Cupid,
Donner and Blitzen. And not to
forget: Rudolph.
As you can see, Schmückie
leaves its mark here too. Everywhere it sparkles sweetly and
shines in all colors. The reindeer also love the Christmas
decorations. They don't want
to be in the stable without
them. Crazy, isn't it?

But have you discovered Kiru here? I haven't found him yet.

But hey ... look! There's Santa's sleigh. Isn't it magical and beautiful?

Come on, let's take a closer look at his sled.

Santa's sleigh is full of surprises. Of course, we can't reveal all the secrets - but we can tell you one thing! Making marshmallows and hot chocolate are just two of the great features that the sleigh hides. A really cool thing.

Incidentally, only Santa Claus is allowed to drive the sleigh. No one else is allowed to get too close.

All right, except for Saubie perhaps. He's a trained cleaning elf. He takes care of the cleaning of the entire Christmas village, as well as the maintenance of the sleigh. When repairs are needed, Saubie is just the man for the job.

Santa has been entrusting Saubie with the sleigh for almost four hundred years now. And so far, nothing has ever gone wrong. That's what I call a great working atmosphere between boss and employee.

Do your parents have such a cool boss?

Cleanliness and cheerfulness,
Saubie is always ready.
He turns and hammers, screws
and wipes,
even removes the chewing gum
from under every table.

Saubie is the janitor elf.

No matter what has broken,
Sau- bie repairs everything.

And if something gets dirty,
Saubie cleans it up.

Tailoring and knitting

Too bad we didn't find Kiru.

I would love to introduce you to Santa Claus, but unfortunately I'm not allowed to.

But I believe that you could only see him like that if he would let you.

Our boss is under constant stress just before Christmas Eve.
Not even the elves get to see him.

On December 24, Santa Claus pays us a brief visit.
He gives a speech first.
Then he swings onto his big, magical sleigh and whizzes around the world at shooting star speed to give all the children plenty of presents.

Can you still remember Kiru's description?
We didn't find him in the library. He wasn't in the stable either.

All that's left for us now is the tailoring shop and the *Treff zur Leckerei.*

The tailor's shop is right next
door. Come on, let's have a
look around.

Off the peg,
We don't have that.
We are elves
and know how to help us.
The tailor's shop, a beautiful
place,
bad taste is far away here.

Have a look around and see if
you can find anyone who fits
Kiru's description.

And if Josie or another elf ad-
dresses you, please don't forget
your name. Your name is Zwölfie!

Here in the tailor's shop they make the most amazing dresses, jackets, pants, hats and much more. Josie and the other elves are true masters in their field.

If you own a warm, fluffy scarf, or your mommy, daddy or a friend of yours does, then it's probably from elf Jo- she. She loves cuddly clothes and invents the most amazing things every year.

The noise here in the Schneiderei is debatable. I find it pretty loud, but I think you get used to the noise.
The sewing machines and the towing machine that produce the soft fabric make a lot of noise.

The singing of Christmas carols, on the other hand, could be
even louder. That doesn't bother
me at all.
Now I've told you so much
again.
I'm a real chatterbox - and we
still haven't found Kiru.
Are you actually bothered by all
my chatter?
Great!
And if you do, please forgive
me!
Now let's quickly continue
our search.
All that's left for us now is the
meeting place for the treat. If we
can't find Kiru there, then I don't
know what to do.
Come on, let's get going,
Twelveie.

Pub talks

This is now the last port of call we have, Zwölfie.

As we walked through the market square and past the big Christmas tree, I thought for a moment that I had seen Kiru.

But that was probably just my imagination.

If Kiru isn't here in the pub either, I really don't know where else we could find the elf.

He's actually here every day and plays rummy with a few elves.

Do you know the card game?

Let's go in!

Kiru is our best card player. He wanted to smuggle himself into Las Vegas last year. He wanted to play against professionals at Caesar's Palace, the famous casino. He had seen it on TV and was immediately hooked.
But Santa wouldn't allow that, and Kiru knows that too.
And Santa sees, hears and knows EVERYTHING!

Oh, wait a minute ...

Look there, Zwölfie. Back there at the bar, in the corner. Vest, red scarf around your neck. I think we've come to the right place.

Yes, indeed! This is Kiru!

"Gosh, that I find you find you here, Kiru!"
"What's wrong, Christmas book?"
"I've been looking for you everywhere.
We need to talk!"
"Then speak, dear book!"
"May me introduce? This is Zwölfie. He's a human."
"What, a human? Are you crazy, Christmas book?"

Zwölfie, have a look around the Treff if you like, while I continue talking to Kiru. But be careful.
"I ended up with this nice child after being moldy in a disgusting cellar for a long time. And the child helped me to find you."

"Oh, dear Christmas book, I was really sad when you disappeared! Father Christmas is on his way to the post office right now. You wouldn't believe what's happened here. We've hardly received any wish lists for months. And the list of naughty children is getting longer and longer, which can only be down to mischief."

"What?! Are you serious, Kiru?"

"Yes, fewer and fewer children still believe in Father Christmas. That's so terribly sad and we can't let that happen."

"But what can we do, Kiru?"

"Be careful, the magic of Christmas night must not disappear!

When the magic of Christmas is gone, we'll be gone too. Not you either, dear Christmas book. You are the reason why we are here at all. This simply must not happen. You have to help us!"
"But how?"
"I'll allow you to stay with the child. But please make sure that the children believe in Santa Claus and us elves again."
"Will do, my friend! Twelveie and I will help you. Every child can read me. But I still have one question. Why was I in the cellar?"
"I can tell you that, my dear. Schabernack has struck again."
"What? Don't say -"

"Yes, dear Christmas book. That fluffy troublemaker had cast the forget-me spell on us. Fortunately, Santa was able to undo the spell. Just a little too late!"

Did you hear that, Zwölfie? A lot of children, including some of your friends, no longer believe in Santa Claus and our magical kingdom.
How can that be?
Christmas means spending a contemplative and magical time. Magic and love are in the air on this night. Children's eyes light up in equal measure, whether rich or poor.

Everyone sings carols while they decorate the Christmas trees and hang the most beautiful Christmas baubles on the fir branches. Peace settles in every room and even the worst quarrels come to an end. Cosiness and tranquillity return, no-one should be alone.

How can you no longer believe in Santa Claus?

Even if you humans can't see the man with the beard, that doesn't mean he doesn't exist. You can't see love with your eyes either - and yet it is there. You can't feel or hear love. Your parents love you. You love your parents. Love is omnipresent, just like Santa Claus.

The wonder of Christmas is a mysterious time.

The earth is silent. In the houses and apartments, a warmth rises through the rooms that enchants everyone's hearts.

And these feelings accompany us here every day.

People must not stop believing in us and remain silent.

We have to do something about this nonsense.

We've known each other for so long now, Zwölfie. We've become close friends.

Come on, let's get the list of good and naughty children. Every child must believe and must not forget.
And until then, please promise me that if you close me up right now to go to your warm bed, then from now on, DO talk about me.
Tell everyone that you have me, the Christmas book, and that I exist.
Tell everyone where I've taken you.
And if your friends don't believe you, they're welcome to read me for themselves!

But first of all, I wish you a peaceful Christmas with your family.

See you next evening!

Your enchanted Christmas book

End

What, you don't want the book to end? Hm. What do you think about **coloring in** a little more and creating your own little colorful Christmas world?

Lilly Kahle from class 9d at the Ulrich von Hutten School in Halle an der Saale has drawn some great pictures. And now you can color them in with your favorite colors.

So take some colored pencils, and on it goes.

Bücher
Leer
Bitte leise sein!!

So, now you've really reached
the end!

www.ingramcontent.com/pod-product-compliance
Lightning Source LLC
LaVergne TN
LVHW021319200726
843509LV00002B/79